Original title:
Moss and Mystery

Copyright © 2025 Creative Arts Management OÜ
All rights reserved.

Author: Ethan Prescott
ISBN HARDBACK: 978-1-80567-247-0
ISBN PAPERBACK: 978-1-80567-546-4

Tapestry of Secrets in the Grove

In the shade where whispers creep,
Frogs wear glasses, the secrets keep.
Trees gossip in a leafy lounge,
Dancing squirrels all around the bounds.

A raccoon with a top hat struts,
Plotting schemes with silly nuts.
Twisted roots that laugh and play,
Beneath the surface, jokes on display.

Shrouded in Nature's Caress

Where shadows play a game of peek,
A shy snail hums a little sneak.
Dandelions tickle the breeze,
While butterflies plot with expert ease.

An owl wears spectacles too wide,
Reading tales with little pride.
Ladybugs trade their polka dots,
In a world where all is not what it spots.

Hidden Layers of the Woodland

Beneath the bark, a party's held,
Where hedgehogs dance, and jokes are melded.
A chorus of crickets sings a tune,
While fireflies flash like stars at noon.

Round and round the mushrooms spin,
Silly capers with a goofy grin.
In the quiet of the leafy fold,
Laughter echoes, stories untold.

The Quiet Pulse of Life

Under the ferns, where oddities grow,
A turtle plays chess with a crow.
Whimsical whispers on the breeze,
As chipmunks jest with tangled keys.

A pilgrimage of ants in suits,
Trotting along in their shiny boots.
The rhythm of leaves, a gentle beat,
In the hilarity of retreat.

Where Silence Grows

In the corner a sock, perfectly alone,
Soft whispers of dust, where no one has grown.
A trampoline of shadows, they bounce with delight,
Socks throw a party, when there's no one in sight.

Lichen throws confetti, in shades of green lace,
Inside jokes with the stones, they laugh at the space.
A giggle from granite, a wink from the floor,
They roast the old roots, behind the closed door.

Invisible creatures play hide and seek well,
With rumors of rumbles, they silently dwell.
The walls have a chatter, it tickles the trees,
Banshees may giggle, but never do sneeze.

Squirrel's high comedy, with acorns in play,
They draft up their scripts in a fanciful way.
With characters trembling, their secrets unfold,
In the quest for the missing, like lost bits of gold.

Tapestries of the Unnoticed

A blanket of fluff lies so soft on the ground,
Teasing the feet with a tickle abound.
The whispers of shadows play hopscotch and cheer,
While ants in top hats parade without fear.

Pinecones in stanzas recite from the trees,
As stillness turns witty, and rustles with ease.
The wind's little giggle, a slap on the back,
Squirrels throw a dance party, in fuzzy wool pack.

Beneath the sly snickers of twigs on a limb,
A chorus of chuckles outglows the dim.
The crickets debating the best time to sing,
Make life a fine puzzle, where weirdness takes wing.

A treasure map drawn with quirk and delight,
With all the odd corners that twinkle at night.
Unraveled connections where laughter can weave,
The fabric of oddness is what we believe.

Hidden Gleam

In the shadows, secrets bloom,
Underneath the forest's gloom.
Pixies dance on little toes,
While squirrels argue 'bout their clothes.

A treasure map made of green and brown,
Leads to giggles all around.
What lies beneath the leafy ferns?
A stash of nuts or just some worms?

Nuturing Secrets

Whispers float on breezy trails,
Where laughter hides and mischief sails.
Beneath the layers, stories sprout,
As rabbits gossip, hopping about.

Comfy homes beneath the trees,
With doors of bark and roofs of leaves.
Each nook a tale, a punchline shared,
While owl in office looks unimpaired.

Between the Leaves

A riddle wrapped in green so bright,
Leaves chuckle softly, tickling light.
A gnome peeks out with a cheeky grin,
As silly squirrels begin their spin.

Under canopies, laughter rings,
As beetles march on tiny wings.
Why does the toad wear polka dots?
To blend in here, or just for laughs and knots?

The Veiled History

Buried deep in grassy lore,
Lie tales of antics yawned before.
With every twist, the humor grows,
Like comic strips from ages woes.

A tickled breeze cries out its jest,
Who'll join the folly? Who's the best?
While nature grins with timeless flair,
At every turn, we find a snare.

Cradle of Whispers Under the Canopy

Beneath the leaves where shadows play,
A leaf-blush bunny hops away.
In secret corners, giggles ring,
As squirrels debate the best nut bling.

The branches sway, a silent jest,
A turtle's shell is surely blessed.
With lichen wigs, they prance around,
In their own world, serene and sound.

Emerald Puzzles of the Ancient Trees

Barks with freckles and tales to share,
A wise old owl grooms its feathered hair.
The whispers twist like tales once told,
Where acorns drop, mischief unfolds.

A raccoon ballet on twiggy toes,
While ants in suits aim for the rose.
Beneath the greenness, secrets thrive,
In the comedy of the wild they strive.

Echoes of an Enchanted Glade

In a realm where the ferns dance,
A toad hums tunes, given a chance.
The mushrooms giggle in polka dot cheer,
As fireflies flash like disco balls near.

Butterflies twirl, auditioning flair,
While spiders weave tales of a delicate snare.
With sap-sweet laughter, the echoes roam,
In this joyful land, they all call home.

The Loom of Time and Greenery

The old stones chuckle, aged yet spry,
As vines weave tales, oh me, oh my!
Every knot holds a story so grand,
Of mischievous winds that tease the land.

Beneath the shade, a tickle of sun,
Where critters gather and all have fun.
Each rustle chimes a merry tune,
In the patchwork quilt of an afternoon.

The Soft Embrace of Nature's Quilt

In the forest's cozy nook,
Lies a blanket, nature's book.
Squirrels giggle, planning schemes,
While rabbits nap in leafy dreams.

Frogs croak jokes by the stream's edge,
Plotting pranks, just a smidge.
The trees chuckle in soft green,
Nature's humor, always seen.

Lost Legends Among the Ferns

Wandering through the leafy maze,
Whispers echo from ancient days.
A wise old turtle shares his tales,
While dancing ants do tiny gales.

The ferns wave like they know a secret,
Encouraging bees to go and tweet it.
Lost legends start to jive and spin,
As giggles rise, and all join in.

Softened Paths in the Gloaming

As twilight wraps the world in fun,
Crickets play, their day's work done.
A raccoon dons his evening hat,
And steals a snack from a friendly cat.

The shadows dance, the fireflies blink,
As creatures gather for a drink.
Together they share a laugh or two,
In the dimming light, under skies so blue.

Green Silhouettes and Silent Stories

In the stillness, shadows play,
From dawn to dusk, they dance away.
A ladybug, a daring spy,
Flies high, plotting, soaring sky-high.

While crickets strum their evening song,
The world's a stage and they belong.
With every chirp, a tale unfolds,
In the hush of green, so brave and bold.

Tales Written in the Grit of Earth

In the dirt, where secrets play,
Pickles dance and squirrels sway.
Lizards wear their polka dots,
While ants debate on tiny plots.

Underneath the rocks they scheme,
Beneath the surface, dreams take steam.
Frogs in coats sip funky tea,
While beetles boast of who's the bee.

Sticks are bartering for a snack,
Trading crumbs on a leafy track.
With giggles shared in quiet cheer,
The soil holds tales we can't quite hear.

Nature's Cryptic Palette

With colors mixed in chaotic glee,
Sassy blooms roll their eyes at bees.
The grass whispers with playful tones,
Tickling toes and sneaky stones.

In the brush, a ruckus brews,
As vibrant hues sing out the blues.
Paint splatters make a mess of trees,
While wind composes silly melodies.

Lavenders giggle, violets cheer,
All in a bicker like it's no fear.
A canvas dressed in earthy charm,
With nature's brush, it's full of barm!

Driftwood Dreams and Dappled Light

Wandering logs with tales to tell,
Chasing shadows where crickets dwell.
Twirling sunbeams dance on bark,
Echoing laughter in the dark.

Driftwood shaped like a quirky chair,
Home for spiders with style to spare.
They sip on dew from morning's cup,
Planning parties till the sun's up.

Whimsical winds tiptoe by,
Whispering jokes to a passing sky.
Each twist and knot a giggly twist,
In the land of wood, you can't resist!

The Gathering of Hidden Beings

In a nook, where laughter came,
Little critters call a name.
A hedgehog juggles acorn hats,
As fireflies debate with bats.

Gather round for a feast of crumbs,
Where butterflies hum silly drums.
A banquet made of twigs and lace,
With doodled maps for a better place.

Fungi wear their finest clothes,
Superb delights, I dare suppose.
The sky tops it all with a chuckle bright,
In the hug of night, all feels just right.

Underfoot Wonders

A carpet of green stretches far and wide,
Poking toes in the fluff, oh, what a ride!
The frogs laugh hard, now where's their throne?
Crossing this plush land, I feel like a knave.

Silly squirrels scurry, with acorns galore,
They slip and they trip, it's a giggly chore.
Leaves shimmy and shake, a dance of delight,
What if the shrooms threw a party tonight?

Twirling around in this magical place,
The ground tickles toes, a comical space.
Time plays tricks as I leap and I bound,
Underfoot wonders, oh joy to be found!

Mystic Greenery

In a land where the greens wear hats made of dew,
Leprechauns plotting a heist, who knew?
With giggles and whispers, the fairies convene,
Turning leaves into crowns, they are quite the scene.

Dancing and prancing under limbs so grand,
The jokes in the woods are all perfectly planned.
A somersault toad hops straight into the fray,
Chasing his tail, he's gone in a sway.

Blades of grass chuckle as I tiptoe by,
Wondering if I might join the nearby spry.
Echoes of laughter drift soft on the breeze,
An adventure awaits, so come if you please!

Beneath the Ancient Boughs

Beneath the old trees with branches that twist,
I stumble on secrets not easily missed.
A fox in sunglasses adjusts his cool stance,
While a snail in a top hat prepares for a dance.

The owls gossip softly, a squabble on high,
They judge my fashion, that sparkle in my eye.
With armfuls of ferns, a creature appears,
Cracking jokes with the flow of the passing years.

A low chuckle erupts from the roots of the trees,
Whispers of jest weave through the leaves in the breeze.
Such silliness thrives in the thick, rustic zone,
Who knew ancient woods could feel like a home?

The Veiled Pathways

Winding through greenery, the pathways unfold,
With quirks and convulsions, odd tales to be told.
A hedgehog in slippers rolls up for a chat,
Offering directions with a tip of his hat.

Between giggles and gasps, the odd ones appear,
A cloak of hilarity drapes over here.
With shadows that dance and alleys that tease,
The paths hold surprises that tickle and please.

I stumble, I laugh, on this zig-zagging way,
A chorus of critters with roles in the play.
Each corner I turn, an odd sight in store,
Forget the map, oh there's always much more!

Secrets Buried in the Softness

In a land where whispers dwell,
A critter hides beneath the swell.
With tiny feet and twitching nose,
He guards the secrets no one knows.

A treasure map made of green fluff,
He giggles, 'This is quite enough!'
While raindrops tap a merry tune,
He dances under the brightening moon.

The Path Less Traveled in Shadow

Down a crooked path so wide,
Curious things, they like to hide.
A squirrel with a monocle and flair,
Proclaims, 'Adventure? Come if you dare!'

In shadows thick where the odd things jive,
Where mushrooms murmur and crickets thrive.
He stops and winks while sipping tea,
'What a curious world this is to see!'

The Soft Underbelly of Time

Time tiptoes on a feathered leaf,
Pausing to share its playful grief.
With tick-tock laughter that fills the air,
It tricks the sun without a care.

Beneath the surface, tales unwind,
Of ancient laughs and secrets twined.
A giggle here, a chuckle there,
Who knew the past could be so rare?

Verdant Veils and Wandering Souls

In a forest draped in leafy glee,
A band of ghosts plays hide and seek.
With playful nudges and cheeky grins,
They jostle 'round like old lost twins.

The veils they wear are fluffy green,
With pranks and jokes that haven't been seen.
They muse, 'Life's a jest, come share a laugh,
In the grand play, be sure to craft!'

Enchanted Growth

In the woods, the green whispers,
Frogs in tuxedos dance with glee.
Squirrels tell tales of vain blunders,
As mushrooms giggle by the tree.

Lichen wears hats made of dew,
While snails ponder their grand escapes.
A rabbit with shoes, oh how it flew,
Through the ferns and all their shapes.

Murmurs in the Dark

The shadows chuckle, secrets unfold,
A hedgehog plays cards with a mouse.
The moonlight spills liquid gold,
As fireflies prank in the house.

Beneath the underbrush, giggles creep,
A raccoon tells stories of old.
Cautious tales that make one leap,
While gnomes stand guard, brave and bold.

Verdant Secrets

Beneath every leaf, a joke does hide,
A worm claims it's the king of night.
While shy mushrooms blush in their pride,
And plants pull pranks out of sight.

Vines weave tales, twisted and fun,
As beetles boast of their racing skills.
Pinecones chuckle under the sun,
In this realm of giggly thrills.

The Calm Before the Thicket

Before the storm, the leaves conspire,
A squirrel juggles acorns with ease.
The rabbits, in fright, form a choir,
While crickets play tunes in the breeze.

Clouds roll in, yet laughter prevails,
As roots tell stories of times gone by.
The breeze tickles plants with its gales,
Before the rain makes them sigh.

Enigmatic Tales from the Thicket

In the thicket, shadows play,
Wiggly worms dance in dismay.
A squirrel in a tiny hat,
Pretends to be a fancy cat.

Beneath the leaves, a secret stash,
Of acorns gone, oh what a crash!
The raccoon laughs, it's quite the sight,
His treasure chest? Just crumbs and light.

The Silent Watchers of the Woods

The trees are gossiping, oh my,
While owl snickers from high up nigh.
A hedgehog rolls, then trips and spins,
He swears he saw a ghostly grin.

Chipmunks chuckle, what a flap,
It's only fungi in a nap!
With twinkling eyes and tiny feet,
They plot to prank the forest's beat.

Lush Shadows

In shadows lush, a snail takes flight,
With borrowed wings – what a delight!
He lands on toadstools that sing tunes,
And hosts a meeting with the raccoon.

The sun peeks in to hear them jest,
While ferns make hats, it's quite the fest!
A foggy dance, a cheeky breeze,
Collapsing giggles, oh do as you please!

Veiled Whispers

Behind the leaves, secrets are stowed,
A rabbit slips on a muddy road.
He fixes his tie, quite a sight to see,
"Today I'll charm that lady bee!"

The hedgehogs murmur, they've much to say,
As crickets wink, joining the play.
With whispers soft and snickers light,
They craft a world of pure delight.

The Art of Disguise

In the forest, shadows loom,
Creatures tiptoe, making room.
A squirrel dons a leafy hat,
While a turtle plays the chatty brat.

A hedgehog might just wear a crown,
As rabbits in suits waddle around.
With style and grace, they all parade,
In this grand game of charades.

Depths of the thicket

In twigs and leaves, secrets lie,
Where a frog croaks a lullaby.
Worms wear glasses, reading maps,
While sloths conduct the forest naps.

A sneaky fox gives quite a wink,
To the owl who's lost in a drink.
Beneath the branches, odd things soar,
Who knew the thicket held such lore?

Curved Paths of Green

The winding paths are never straight,
Each turn reveals a quirky fate.
Snails race in a slippery spree,
Cheering loudly, 'You can't catch me!'

A mushroom wears a dapper tie,
While butterflies laugh as they fly by.
With every step, the giggles grow,
In the green veils, merriment flows.

The Breath of the Forest

In whispers, trees share their dreams,
As the wind plays playful schemes.
Raccoons dance with zany flair,
While panda bears sit in mid-air.

The breeze tells jokes, and leaves clap hands,
Quirky antics fill the lands.
With every rustle, laughter blends,
In this breath where joy never ends.

Secrets Beneath the Canopy

In the shade where whispers play,
Frogs in bowties leap and sway.
A squirrel with secrets tickles the air,
While owls wear glasses like they just don't care.

The acorns dance, a goofy parade,
As the trees gossip, unafraid.
Beneath this green, what oddities dwell?
Perhaps a fairy with a ticklish spell.

Rabbits in coats, a fashion delight,
Nibble on snacks through the moonlit night.
With every rustle, a chuckle arises,
Nature's jesters, in clever disguises.

So next time you stroll in the shady glen,
Remember the laughter, again and again.
For under each leaf, and behind every stump,
Are tales of humor, in nature's great rump.

Emerald Enigma

In the forest's embrace, a riddle unfolds,
With whispers of laughter that no one beholds.
A turtle in shades, struts with a grin,
While the hedgehogs find parties where mischief begins.

Lurking in shadows, a cat's tiny feet,
Stumble on mushrooms, oh what a feat!
The owls keep watch, with their wise nighttime glee,
As snippets of antics fill up the tree.

Beneath leafy blankets, odd puzzles await,
A garden of giggles, an unusual state.
Bumblebees buzzing, with jokes in their flight,
Creating a symphony of silly delight.

So take a good look at the green tapestry,
Laughter is woven in every debris.
For in every nook, a chuckle you'll find,
The whimsical world where spirits unwind.

Soft Cover of Time

Under layers of quilted leaves,
A subtitle of chuckles and playful thieves.
Whiskers of secrets dive under the ground,
As mushrooms hold meetings, all gathered around.

Twirling and whirling, the frogs put on shows,
Ribbits in rhythm, everyone knows.
A snail in a top hat keeps time with his shell,
While snickering shadows weave tales they won't tell.

Lichens are artists, painting the rocks,
With colors inspired by past paradox.
The ants conduct symphonies without any care,
While critters take claps in a forest encore fair.

So peek through the branches, where laughter's entwined,
Each petal, a story, a twist you've defined.
For under the soft cover of days gone by,
Are giggles and glee that forever will fly.

Forgotten Trails

On paths where the strange likes to stroll,
With fluffs and puffs, the air is a troll.
A raccoon in boots, struts with great flair,
As hedgehogs play tag with wild, tangled hair.

Sunlight drips down like honey on bread,
With whispers of snacks that the creatures have fed.
Fungi in tophats host parties at dawn,
While gnomes crack up in their little green lawn.

Jokes of the forest drifting along,
With songs of the night, a most silly throng.
The berries are chuckling, all ripe for the play,
In the heart of the wild, come join the ballet.

So wander these trails where the quirky convene,
And notice the giggles in every shade of green.
For when you get lost, just follow the cheer,
And giggle along with all nature's veneer.

Secrets of the Forest Floor

In the woods where whispers play,
Tiny creatures laugh all day.
A clump of green, who could it be?
A gnome with tea and a dancing bee?

Beneath the ferns and aged bark,
Lives a squirrel who loves to spark.
With acorns hoarded, he starts to scheme,
Wielding a spoon for a nutty dream!

Rocky boots shuffle with glee,
Who's spying on this jubilee?
A rabbit in shades, very hip,
Sips carrot juice, takes a sip!

So tiptoe lightly, lend an ear,
To giggles shared from far and near.
The forest floor, a lively show,
Where secrets bounce and laughter flows.

Hidden Life

Underfoot, a world so wild,
Where not one leaf is ever mild.
A bug in boots breaks into dance,
While mushrooms giggle, take a chance!

In this brush, a party thrives,
With critters jiving, oh, how they strive!
A snail spins tales on a tiny stage,
While ants play cards, their ace a rage!

Hare brings snacks, he's quite the chef,
Crafts a salad from his left-of-wrest.
Every turn, new sights to share,
In nature's club, the fun is rare!

Every step reveals a friend,
In this place where giggles blend.
So come along, don't hesitate,
Join the fun, it's never late!

The Unseen Tapestry

A web of secrets woven tight,
With each thread dancing in delight.
Pine cones chuckle, twirling 'round,
As mushrooms giggle on the ground.

An owl winks, a playful tease,
While fireflies throw a disco spree.
Leaves rustle jokes, they can't resist,
Nature's humor in every twist!

A chattering woodpecker in a hat,
Knocks on trees for a gossip chat.
Squirrels flipping like acrobats,
Leave us chuckling at their spats!

With every inch of fertile earth,
Lies a party of endless mirth.
So stroll along this secret lane,
Where the unseen wraps joy in its vein.

Cryptic Growth

In the shade where shadows creep,
Lies a riddle for us to keep.
A patch of green laughs, 'What's the fuss?'
As bees in bowties collect the dust!

A snail debates a slug in jest,
"Who grows faster? Let's take a rest!"
With each step, the funky roots,
Are planning parties with fancy suits!

Tangled vines twist in delight,
Playing tag from morning to night.
Fungi paint smiles on the floor,
Saying, "Join us! There's always more!"

So peer below, don't miss the game,
In this odd place, it's never same.
Nature's laughter sprouts and glows,
In a place where fun surely grows!

Secrets of Sunlit Glades

In the woods where secrets hide,
Frogs wear ties and bugs take pride.
With whispers soft and giggles near,
Even stones might shed a tear.

The squirrels dance in silly shoes,
While butterflies plot their next big ruse.
Each rustle holds a chuckle tight,
As shadows leap with pure delight.

A rabbit's wiggle, a raccoon's grin,
The sunlight knows where games begin.
Ticklish ferns that twirl and sway,
In the glades where jesters play.

So come and laugh where secrets bloom,
In every crevice, there's room for zoom.
The world is bright, and life's a jest,
Here in the glade, we're simply blessed.

Realm of the Unseen

In corners dark, where no one peeks,
Live cheeky sprites with funny cheeks.
They throw confetti made of dreams,
And giggle softly, or so it seems.

Invisible friends swing on a thread,
With whispered secrets, they're easily led.
They play hide and seek with passing winds,
Crafting laughter as the day begins.

The air is thick with magical fun,
Where laughter lingers like rays of sun.
If you listen close, you might just hear,
The chuckles of beings that linger near.

In this realm, where sights deceive,
And nothing's ever what you believe,
Let your heart take flight and soar,
In the unseen world, there's always more.

Shadows of the Past

Shadows tiptoe in the dusk,
With silly hats and a hint of musk.
They share old tales of clumsy falls,
And squeaky shoes in bustling halls.

Those echoes chuckle in the breeze,
As laughter dances through the trees.
The wisps of yore hold fun and grace,
In every nook, there's a smiling face.

Old ghosts gather round for a spree,
Trading tales of their wild glee.
A twist of fate, a slide of chance,
In twilight's glow, they all prance.

So heed the whispers from the way back,
In shadows past, no laughter lacks.
With every step, let joy amass,
In the playful dance of glimmers vast.

Cradle of the Forgotten

In a cradle where lost things sleep,
Old toys giggle, secrets they keep.
Forgotten hats and jumping jacks,
They plot to prank those coming back.

With a wobbly tune and a creaky song,
They reel you in, you can't go wrong.
Dust bunnies tumble, sharing a joke,
In this haven, where laughter awoke.

Cobwebs sway to the rhythm of cheer,
While crumpled maps lead adventurers near.
Each corner holds a vibrant riddle,
As laughter echoes, soft yet brittle.

So visit the cradle, take a chance,
Where the forgotten enjoy their dance.
In the heart of stillness, joy will latch,
In a world of whimsy, no one will snatch.

The Enchantment of Silence

In the quiet grove, gnomes take tea,
Whispering secrets of a tree.
Their hats are tall, their shoes are bright,
Dancing shadows in the night.

A squirrel chuckles, it rolls on the ground,
While fairies giggle, no one's around.
A toad croaks out, with a wink and a grin,
Join our party, let the fun begin!

Strange things linger among the roots,
Root beer flows, and it's wearing boots.
The ghost of a cat plays hide-and-seek,
With a bag of tricks, oh what a cheek!

Under bright cap mushrooms they twirl,
Spinning in circles, oh what a whirl!
And as we laugh, in the moon's soft glow,
What secrets the night might still hold, we don't know!

Green Dreams

A wizard with a scruffy old beard,
Summons a frog that has no fear.
It croaks a tune that's slightly off-key,
As the hedgehogs sway in glee.

Ducking behind ferns with flair,
The lizards gossip without a care.
They claim the earth's a dance floor grand,
Where flowers nod and insects band.

Bubbles of laughter float through the air,
As critters compete in a wacky affair.
A snail slides by, thinking it slick,
While a witty bug tells a joke, real quick!

And in the mist, secrets do bloom,
With each silly twist, we giggle and fume.
In dreams of green, where humor blooms wide,
Laughter and nature, forever abide.

Beneath the Green Shroud

In the forest depths, where shadows creep,
A dance of the odd makes the liveliest heap.
Beetles in bow ties, with swagger and flair,
Fling each other about without a care.

A hedgehog juggles acorns with ease,
While chatting with owls, up high in the trees.
They spin tales of brilliance, both funny and wise,
As raccoons snicker with a glint in their eyes.

Fungi form seats where the critters convene,
Whispers and giggles all sparkling green.
A riddle is posed by a bemused silver hare,
"Why do trees nod? Don't they have a scare?"

Everyone chuckles, as the sun starts to fade,
In this world where laughter is unafraid.
Beneath the green cloak, the odd and the wild,
We dance through the twilight, pure mischief compiled!

Veil of Verdancy

Under a veil of emerald sheen,
Life can be quirky, if you know what I mean.
With tiny trolls in a raucous song,
They're tiny but mighty, come join along!

A dance of the leaves, in a whimsical breeze,
With squirrels in tutus and starlight keys.
Mice recite poems on mushrooms so grand,
While ants in tuxedos take a witty stand.

A beetle, quite sly, starts a conga line,
As the stars twinkle bright, shimmering divine.
The laughter is loud, a riddle takes flight,
"Why did the vine bring a party tonight?"

As the shadows grow long and the moon starts to rise,
A parrot squawks wisdom, in jokes and in lies.
With giggles and glee, we'll celebrate more,
In the whimsical world where oddities soar!

The Poetry of Decay

In the garden, weeds take a stroll,
Dancing slowly, they've found their role.
Old boots line the fence with flair,
Unlaced dreams just hang in the air.

Rotting apples hold meetings at dusk,
Decaying foliage is a must.
They giggle and whisper, it's quite absurd,
In the poetry of decay, words are blurred.

Mushrooms plan picnics, fun-filled and bright,
While worms in tuxedos dance with delight.
Nature's odd soiree, a real hootenanny,
All presided by the old, wise Granny.

Sticks host a party, they're feeling alive,
With party hats fashioned from bark, they thrive.
In twilight's glow, the fun never ends,
Amongst all the weeds, they're the best of friends.

Curiosities of the Underworld

Down below where the wild things dwell,
Giggling gophers cast a magic spell.
They juggle acorns, quite a sight to see,
While snails host races, oh what glee!

Rats in tuxes sip on root beer floats,
A real soirée on subterranean moats.
Hiding treasures from groundhogs and moles,
With secret handshakes, they share their goals.

Ants in a conga line, marching with flair,
Dancing to tunes made of dirt and despair.
Worms throw confetti, but it's just their skin,
New fashion statements, they proudly grin.

In this snazzy den, surprises abound,
Where laughter erupts from the soft, dark ground.
The underworld's quirks, a lively parade,
In a carnival of odd, the fun is displayed.

Whispers of the Woodland

In the forest, leaves wink and weave,
Squirrels in capes plot tricks up their sleeves.
They chatter about a mysterious feast,
Even the grumpy old owl can't cease!

Beneath the roots, fungi share tapes,
Their gossip travels in whimsical shapes.
Foxes wear glasses, they read all the news,
While badgers play bingo, don't they amuse?

Mice in the shadows debate on a plan,
To sneak past the cat—oh, will they, they can!
With acorn hats and a snicker or two,
It's a woodland party, the mischief ensues.

A tree trunk plays jazz, with roots for a band,
The woodpeckers join in, it's grand and unplanned.
Amongst laughter and lights, they dance without cost,
In the whispers of trees, no joy is lost.

Life in the Layers

Beneath the surface, stories unfold,
A snack for the critters, both timid and bold.
Layers of laughter, stories entwine,
Where secrets are buried in places divine.

In muddy puddles, frogs trade old tales,
With crickets adding their whimsical wails.
A log hosts meetings of all kinds,
Where wisdom and laughter are what one finds.

The buzzing of beetles creates quite the jam,
While shy little slugs sing a soft lilting slam.
In the embrace of the earth, joy is profound,
Life thrives in layers, where magic's unbound.

Beneath every stone, there's a jiggle and wiggle,
As creatures partake in a round of the giggle.
Nestled deep down, it's a wild folks' playground,
In life's hidden layers, where fun knows no bound.

The Mystery Beneath

In the forest, secrets creep,
Under leaves where whispers sleep.
What's the creature, stout and round?
Chasing shadows on the ground?

Squirrels plotting with a grin,
Over acorns, they begin.
"Who needs nuts?" a raccoon says,
"Let's start a dance and play all day!"

Behind the trunks, a giggle swells,
Tales of charm the quiet tells.
What's that sparkle, is it real?
Or just a playful nutty deal?

The forest floor, a wild stage,
With critters acting, full of rage.
"Take a bow!" the rabbit cried,
"Dance your way right by my side!"

In the Embrace of Green

Green's a color oh so bright,
Lives a snail with dreams in flight.
"I'll be faster," he declares,
While a tortoise snickers, "Who cares?"

Beneath the canopy so wide,
A lizard dons a leafy guide.
"Fashion's key!" he boasts with pride,
As caterpillars giggle, side by side.

Ducks in hats and frogs in shoes,
Strutting in the morning hues.
"Oops!" said one, with style askew,
"Should have worn my dancing shoes!"

In this realm, absurdity reigns,
Where everyone has funny chains.
Giggling grass and silly trees,
Tickling all the honeybees!

Beneath the Dappled Light

Under sunlight's playful tease,
Dancing shadows, swaying leaves.
A rabbit hops with lightspeed flair,
While ants hold court, a banquet there.

The birds gossip, feathers fluffed,
Mice plot mischief, no time's too tough.
"Who stole the crumbs?" a cheeky crow,
Points to the squirrel with a hearty row.

Beneath a tree, a party brews,
All the critters share their views.
"Let's tell tales!" the raccoon jeered,
"About the snacks that disappeared!"

Then night descends, the moon shines bright,
A whispered laugh, oh what a sight!
The midnight dance of furry crew,
Ends with a hiccup and a "who knew?"

Echoes in the Moss

Deep within a woodland shade,
A ghostly joke the shadows made.
"Boo!" said the mouse, with such a fright,
While owls laughed, "What a funny sight!"

The grounds whisper, "Do you hear?"
Stories tickled, year by year.
"Where's my snack?" the badger said,
As beetles danced above his head.

Timid rabbits, on their guard,
Frogs sing loudly, "Life's not hard!"
With every croak, a burst of cheer,
Making echoes, far and near.

Then laughter rings, a silly sound,
In hidden nooks, where glee is found.
The night is young, so let's all toast,
To silly things we love the most!

Secrets in the Shade

In a hidden nook beneath the trees,
A squirrel whispers secrets to the breeze.
With acorns stacked like little dreams,
They plot a heist, or so it seems.

The shadows giggle, playing hide and seek,
Where sunlight shimmers, soft and sleek.
A dance of leaves, a rustle and twirl,
In the woodland world, a secret whirl.

Fragments of the Forgotten

Old boots left soggy by a rain-filled plop,
With laces knotted like a hilarious stop.
A hat with holes that tells no tales,
Hiding in corners where humor prevails.

Lost umbrellas that pinky promise to fly,
If only they could, oh my, oh my!
Each fragment laughs at the passing years,
As they murmur giggles amongst the peers.

Soft Footfalls

A rabbit hops on tip-toe so sly,
Hiding behind a bush with a wink of an eye.
Its fluffy tail a shaky delight,
In a game of peek-a-boo, all day and night.

Beneath the cover of twinkling stars,
The nighttime critters drive tiny cars.
With squeaks and chuckles, their engines roar,
As soft footfalls greet the forest floor.

Tangled Roots

Roots twist and turn like a playful vine,
Crafting stories of the times divine.
With socks mismatched and shoes untied,
They laugh at the strut of the world outside.

A ticklish stretch beneath the ground,
Where mysteries giggle and twirl around.
In this earthbound maze, they plot and scheme,
For tangled roots know how to dream.

Lush Wonders of the Unseen

In a forest so green, things are awry,
Where whispers are louder than birds in the sky.
A squirrel in a hat, quite the stylish bird,
Critiques all the mushrooms, but we've never heard.

The mushrooms all giggle, they dance with delight,
While crickets debate what is wrong or is right.
A hedgehog arrives with a book in his paws,
Saying, "Sorry for being, such a thorn in your flaws!"

But under a leaf, a secret is spun,
A ladybug's party, oh what a fun run!
With laughter and bubbles, they lighten the gloom,
While rabbits bring snacks, in a whimsical room.

Oh, the stories they share, unwritten but bold,
Of a snail on a mission, with treasure to hold.
In shadows they wander, not a care in their way,
Planting tales of laughter, forever they'll stay.

Hushed Tales of the Underbrush

In the thicket so dense, here's a tale to be told,
Of a critter so cheeky, with antics so bold.
A frog on a lily, singing off-key,
As butterflies snicker, 'What a sight to see!'

The badger's a poet, writing sonnets in mud,
While ants form a band, creating a thud.
They dance to the rhythm, two-step in a line,
While a wise old owl grins, 'Are we lost in time?'

Through the thorns and the brambles, a giggle escapes,
As a family of hedgehogs makes hats out of grapes.
With laughter that echoes, they charm the deep night,
And fireflies blink in, just to see the delight.

A whispering breeze brings secrets galore,
Of a squirrel that swears he once flew off the floor.
But who are we kidding? For all that we've seen,
It's just a raucous forest, full of zest and sheen!

Shadows of Forgotten Footsteps

In the echoing woods, where the daisies do sway,
There are shadows that scuffle, not quite here to play.
A raccoon in a tux, with a pie on his head,
He claims he's the king, and the garden's his bed.

The whispers and giggles of critters abound,
A chorus of nonsense that mixes around.
The rabbits roll laughing, they tumble and flop,
While the hedgehogs keep score with a thistle-top hop.

The forest is full of a quirky parade,
With beetles on scooters, a grand escapade.
They sing all their songs, though a bit out of tune,
As the night sky winks back with a mischievous moon.

Each shadow holds tales of the funny and bright,
Of creatures who flourish in wild, joyful night.
When the stars start to twinkle, 'neath the blanket of trees,
The laughter is endless, carried off by the breeze.

Verdant Echoes in the Twilight

In the twilight's embrace, where oddities grow,
A turtle with glasses says, 'Look at me go!'
He paces quite slow, but he's wisdom embodied,
As the fireflies twirl, with some dance steps, all shoddy.

The brambles all chuckle, they tease the tall grass,
As a hedgehog disco moves, shattering class.
'Oh, what a fine twist!' they snicker and sway,
While a caterpillar hums, in a jazzy array.

The trees lean in closer, to catch every jest,
As the night creatures gather, at their vibrant fest.
A chameleon changes, just to fit in,
While a fox in a bow tie reveals his sly grin.

It's a party for those who throw caution away,
In a banquet of laughter, where friends do not stray.
With echoes of joy, and a pinch of surprise,
In the heart of the twilight, fun never dies!

Forgotten Edges

On a log with a quirky stance,
A critter wobbles, doing its dance.
It twirls and trips, oh what a sight,
Nature's own jester, full of delight.

Beneath the leaves, a riddle's found,
A sandwich left on the cold, wet ground.
The ants throw a party, they munch and cheer,
As their tiny king makes a toast with a sneer.

In shadows where giggles softly breeze,
A snail in a top hat claims to seize.
His slimy reign of the forest floor,
Has everyone laughing, begging for more.

And as the sun dips, the critters shrink,
Whispers below make us stop and think.
What silliness thrives in the damp and dark?
In every nook, there's a giggling spark!

Soft Places

In the cradle of shadows, the soft things breathe,
Finding a bed where the sprawlers weave.
A hedgehog snores in his grassy retreat,
While the snickering fairies tickle his feet.

Under a clump of wild, fuzzy clover,
A grouchy old worm turns over and over.
'This isn't a spa! You kids, go away!'
But the laughs keep coming; he's part of their play.

Mushrooms giggle in polka-dot hats,
As curious beetles perform silly chats.
They tumble and roll in the sweet, earthy gloom,
Creating a ruckus, they fill up the room.

And as twilight descends, they smirk in the shade,
In soft places where visions parade.
The world is a circus, no need to disguise,
In the gentle embrace, laughter always lies!

Secrets in the Understory

Beneath the great giants, secrets abound,
Where chompers and munchers strum joyful sounds.
A beetle in shades plays the lead guitar,
As a parade of worms groove from afar.

Ticklish tendrils wave high and low,
Chasing each other, putting on quite a show.
The twisted roots nod, they're part of the crew,
While the squirrels crack jokes, as all good friends do.

A raccoon in shades sneaks in for the feast,
With a snack of leftovers from last night's beast.
He winks at the mushrooms, his buddies in crime,
In the theater of greens, it's always their time.

With giggles and wiggles, they spin through the night,
In the underworld's party, everything's bright.
So keep your ears open, the fun's never done,
For secrets are shared where the wild things run!

Whispers of the Earth

In the depths, where the giggles softly dwell,
There's a ruckus of stories no one can tell.
A grasshopper with flair recites tales so grand,
Of beetle ballrooms, and snail bands at hand.

Tickling whispers roam underfoot,
As roots twist and turn, taking root.
A worm wearing glasses reads old soil maps,
While ants silently giggle, causing their traps.

Beneath every pebble, a secret unfolds,
In the dark, where the jubilant laughter holds.
The stones chuckle back, with a clink and a clank,
As the night whispers jokes in a playful prank.

So next time you wander through leaves and the dew,
Remember the whispers and laughter in view.
For in every crevice, a chuckle finds birth,
In the quiet, cheerful whispers of the earth!

The Silk of Shadows

In the corner of the glade, a secret's twirl,
A dance of whispers, a giggle unfurl.
Who knew that the ferns had so much to share?
All those silly tales floating on air.

A bramble once claimed it wore a top hat,
And the trees laughed at it, 'Look at that!'
A squirrel chimes in, with acorn in paw,
'Of all this nonsense, I'm just in awe!'

A shadowy figure slips by with a grin,
What could it be? Oh, the curious din.
A rabbit with slippers? A hedgehog in shades?
The rumors around here are never displayed.

With a flick of the leaves, the laughter does rise,
As creatures come forth to unveil their disguise.
The woods are a stage, absurdity reigns,
In this secretive space, fun flows through the veins.

Under the Weight of Time

Time wears a hat that's too big for its head,
It trips on the roots as it spins through the spread.
Tick-tock, tick-tock, the old clock does tease,
Finding lost moments beneath the tall trees.

An owl with a bowtie gives wisdom so grand,
While tortoises giggle, unable to stand.
A sunbeam bursts forth, with a ticklish glow,
As petals fall down in a comical show.

The old tales they tell of a bird that's not here,
One that wears boots made of butter, my dear!
It leaps on the brambles, all hearty and spry,
Filling the air with a sweet-smelling sigh.

Time stumbles and tumbles, what fun can it find?
In the realms of the woods, where laughter's entwined.
Underneath ancient boughs, it performs a ballet,
As giggles and chuckles lead the way.

Veiled in Green

A curtain of leaves, so lush and so bright,
Covers the secrets that dance in plain sight.
What lurks in the shadows? A squeak and a flap,
Turns out it's just a rogue, plotting for a nap!

With hats made of petals and shoes full of mud,
The toads host a party, oh what a flood!
A party of critters, each one with a quirk,
And all of them waiting for the next little jerk.

A chortle erupts from the vines overhead,
As a raccoon teases, 'You snooze, you're misled!'
A giggle, a snort, and then laughter erupts,
In this place woven tight, where joy is corrupt.

Veils of green sway to the rhythm of glee,
With every slight whisper, they're welcoming me.
A silly brigade of winks and sweet sighs,
In this leafy embrace, the laughter just flies.

Boughs and Secrets

Boughs hang low, with secrets to tell,
Birds plotting pranks under the old wishing well.
A giggle escapes from the branches so high,
While squirrels in shades sip their nutty chai.

The trees gossip softly, they play hide and seek,
Telling old tales they share every week.
A fox with a grin sneaks around with a pause,
To catch all the punchlines, without any flaws.

There's a legend of hedgehogs with tiny umbrellas,
Who dance in the moonlight, the quirkiest fellows.
With mischief and mirth written all on their backs,
These laughs in the woods leave us all in the cracks.

So under the boughs, come spin in the cheer,
With whimsy and giggles, let's gather near!
For the secrets of joy are all woven in jest,
In this wild, vibrant nook, we are truly blessed.

The Green Veil

In a forest where whispers play,
Creepy shadows dance all day.
A green cover, so sly and spry,
Like a prankster saying hi!

Underfoot, secrets creep and crawl,
A ticklish tickle that enthralls.
It giggles when you take a step,
A jester's plot, a playful prep!

Goblins peek from their leafy throne,
Tickled by laughter all their own.
Frogs in coats that gleam and shine,
Croak a tune that's truly fine!

So as you wander, take a look,
At this green page, a dancing book.
Each turn a giggle, every glance a tease,
Nature's jesters, just to please!

Hidden in Twilight

When dusk wraps the woods in a shroud,
The giggles of nighttime grow loud.
Creatures clad in a twilight hue,
Play peek-a-boo with a cheeky view!

A squirrel dressed in shades of gray,
Jumps on branches like kids at play.
He hides in shadows, then pops in sight,
With a wink that sparks delight!

Beneath the trees, a riddle brews,
With answers lost among the blues.
Flickering lights, like stars that wink,
Nudge your heart as you start to think!

So tread with care through the darkening light,
Where every rustle is full of fright.
But laughter echoes as you pass by,
In the giggles of who knows why?

Nature's Cloak

Wrapped in layers of lush delight,
A blanket keeps secrets out of sight.
With each step, a smirk awaits,
As nature jests and celebrates!

Beneath the cover, the stories sneak,
With tiny creatures that really peek.
A bouncing bug with a silly face,
Makes the gloom turn into grace!

Gentle whispers of wind have fun,
Playing tag before the sun.
A cranky branch may hide and sway,
In jest, it blocks your sunny play!

So venture forth with a giggling heart,
In this riddle where all things start.
Embrace the laughter, let it flow,
In nature's cloak, all jesters grow!

The Silent Watchers

In the quiet corners of the glade,
Lurking shadows share a masquerade.
Eyes peek out from every nook,
Plotting pranks, just take a look!

With every step, a giggle bursts,
As mother nature's plan rehearsed.
With cheeky winds that tease and play,
They dance around in a sly ballet!

Old tree trunks are the laugh-givers,
Telling tales of shivers and slivers.
Caught in the light, they chuckle and sway,
While tiny critters prance and play!

So join the ballet of the whimsical night,
Where the silly shadows give delight.
With each glance, a chuckle awaits,
In the silent watch, where fun creates!

The Allure of Shadows

In the corner, something twitches,
A whisper from the dark that itches.
A sock or two—I really can't tell,
They're dancing about as if under a spell.

A shadow leaps, and then it falls,
Sneakers giggle down the halls.
Is that a cat? Or just a shoe?
No one quite knows—do you have a clue?

A waltz with ghosts, or maybe a prune,
A trickster's banquet under the moon.
With puns in the air like balloons that float,
What's lurking beneath? Just a lively coat!

So take a step into the night,
Where oddities dance and things feel right.
With laughter echoing in the corner,
You'll find surprises, a bit of a foreigner.

Flourish in the Gloom

In the attic, a sage that sings,
A toe-tapping broom, oh the joy it brings!
With a whiff of old cheese, and dust in a blink,
Beware of the goblins—don't stop to think!

They twirl around with feathered hats,
Sipping from cups shaped like little rats.
Where did they come from, this merry crew?
With a wink and a nod, they've invited you.

Wobble and jiggle, embrace the gloom,
Let the chuckles chase away the doom.
For every cobweb, a story will spin,
And laughter is found where the odd begins.

So dance with the shadows, have a great time,
Life's just a riddle, a preverbal rhyme.
With candlesticks laughing and winks on the sly,
Who knew the dark could be such a guy?

The Lure of the Hidden

Under the steps where whispers swell,
A treasure awaits in a secret shell.
What's in there—thoughts of cheese?
Or perhaps a feast for the wandering bees?

Creak and rattle, the hinges creak,
A chest that giggles, a sense of the chic.
Is that a trinket or an old shoe?
With mysteries waiting, a joke or two.

What lives in shadows? A deck of cards,
Or maybe a frog with a set of regards?
A laugh in the dark, a ruckus undone,
Makes even the shadows hop about for fun.

So push the door and step right in,
To find a court jester with a silly grin.
With tales aplenty from the deep and wide,
Join the carnival, take a whimsical ride!

Forgotten Echoes

In the corners where the memories lay,
Chortles and giggles refuse to decay.
Echoes of yesteryears filled with cheer,
What's that old saying? "Always speak near!"

Cracks in the paint, a giggle or two,
Maybe some gnomes hiding in blue.
Cabbages rolling and singing a tune,
In forgotten spots beneath the moon.

Stale bread charms and frolicking rye,
Swirling about as if to fly.
With nudges and winks from behind the wall,
It's a party of secrets—come one, come all!

So laugh with the echoes and dance with delight,
For the forgotten ones revel in the night.
In this realm where giggles bloom,
Our sides ache from laughter in every room.

www.ingramcontent.com/pod-product-compliance
Lightning Source LLC
Chambersburg PA
CBHW071849160426
43209CB00003B/480